HOT TUBS & SPAS

Schiffer Publishing Ltd®

4880 Lower Valley Road, Atglen, PA 19310 USA

HOT TUBS & SPAS

An Inspirational Design Guide

Tina Skinner

Acknowledgments

Once again, to the members at staff at the Master Pools Guild, Inc. who shared their work with me to create another inspiring book.

Designed by John P. Cheek
Cover Design by Bruce Waters
Type set in Brush 455 BT/Zurich BT
ISBN: 0-7643-1841-1
Printed in China

Published by Schiffer Publishing Ltd.
4880 Lower Valley Road
Atglen, PA 19310
Phone: (610) 593-1777; Fax: (610) 593-2002
E-mail: Schifferbk@aol.com
Please visit our web site catalog at
www.schifferbooks.com
We are always looking for people to write books on new and related subjects. If you have an idea for a book please contact us at the above address.

This book may be purchased from the publisher.
Include $3.95 for shipping.
Please try your bookstore first.
You may write for a free catalog.

In Europe, Schiffer books are distributed by
Bushwood Books
6 Marksbury Ave.
Kew Gardens
Surrey TW9 4JF England
Phone: 44 (0) 20 8392-8585; Fax: 44 (0) 20 8392-9876
E-mail: Bushwd@aol.com
Free postage in the U.K., Europe; air mail at cost.

Contents

Introduction

Simply looking at a spa seems to lower your blood pressure. Here is a peek into dozens of private backyards and spa rooms for a chance to see firsthand the best in spa design. Members of the Master Pools Guild, Inc. craft water retreats for their clients that are custom designed to suit their individual needs and tastes, and to work in harmony with the architecture of their home and landscape.

The latest technology allows hydrotherapy spas to provide soothing warmth and vigorous jet massage. It also enables the designers to create spas that double as water fountains and waterfalls, making them focal points within a landscape, and adding the relaxing sound of falling water to the healthful benefits of a spa investment.

In the initial stages of planning a spa, homeowners will want to consider their needs. How many people will use the spa will help determine how big the spa needs to be and how much seating is needed in the water. They may wish to build a home addition to house the spa indoors, or they may prefer to soak under the stars. They may want to make the spa part of a garden setting, disguising it as a reflecting pool or small pond. Or they may want to make it part of a larger swimming and entertaining complex. Further, they will want to consider textures and colors, both of the spa lining, the spa surround, and the patio or environment where the spa will be housed.

Examples for all of these are contained herein. This book is an excellent opportunity to explore the wide range of stone, concrete, brick, and tile options available without visiting dozens of showrooms. It is an opportunity for all the members of the household to share their tastes and opinions, and to help form a consensus before approaching a contractor to work out the final details.

More than being a practical tool, however, this book is a miniature fantasy escape, a virtual indulgence. It is hard to turn these pages without picturing yourself in them, and lingering there. Enjoy!

Gem-like Settings

Geometric stones create two tiers up to a circular, blue-tile spa.
Courtesy of Hollandia Pools & Spas

Glass block creates a transparent wall between spa and pool waters, mixed with the motion of falling water off a negative edge. The flick of a switch turns off the waterfall and the spa waters are piping warm in 30 minutes or less. The tile trim is a photo image of river rock.
Courtesy of Aqua Blue Pools

Boulders and evergreens add a wall of privacy beyond a perfectly circular spa. *Courtesy of Gib-San Pools, Ltd.*

A circular spa offers raised seating for fully clothed pool-side party go-ers, as well as sunken seating for those in need of repose. *Courtesy of Memphis Pool Supply Company*

Concrete is an economical, and durable, alternative to stone, with coloring and imprinting techniques that are almost indistinguishable from Nature's designs. *Courtesy of Terry Pool Company, Inc.*

Evergreens and a half-wall of brick form a semi-circle of privacy around a spa.
Courtesy of Terry Pool Company, Inc.

A strip of walled patio hugs the home tightly, culminating in a circular spa.
Courtesy of Rizzo Pool Construction Co.

A spa makes an attractive midpoint in a backyard slope. *Courtesy of Terry Pool Company, Inc.*

A stone retaining wall coordinates with a natural spa surround, and creates a beautiful backdrop. *Courtesy of Alka Pool Construction, Ltd.*

Lighting reflects off border tiles that edge pool and spa.
Courtesy of Shasta Pools & Spas

Raised stone seating provides footing inside or out
of a circular spa. *Courtesy of Gib-San Pools, Ltd.*

A circular spa is raised above the pool on a tile-lined platform. A handrail offers safety for the descent into soothing waters. A spillover can be activated when the spa is not in use for visual and aural effect. *Courtesy of Barrington Pools, Inc.*

Glass block provides a transparent transition from pool to spa. *Courtesy of Panama Pools*

Cut capstones give this spa an air of permanence, augmented by a river stone spillover beyond. *Courtesy of Gib-San Pools, Ltd.*

Colorful tile characterizes a raised spa and pool border. *Courtesy of New Bern Pool*

Stonework supports a raised spa and stairway access. *Courtesy of Mission Pools*

Water circulates around a raised spa, trickling beside elegantly curved stairs and spilling over a narrow channel into a filtration and circulation system. *Courtesy of Mission Pools*

Black adds elegance to a spa, complete with a spillover view for the household occupants.
Courtesy of Shasta Pools & Spas

A stone environment sets the stage for a deep, muscle-relaxing retreat.
Courtesy of Memphis Pool Supply Company

Two tiers define edge and seating in a bean-shaped hydro-therapy spa. An ozone sanitizer is used for water purification, providing minimal chemical usage. *Courtesy of Creative Master Pools*

A key-shaped spa includes stairs for the descent into heaven. *Courtesy of Gib-San Pools, Ltd.*

Besides being attractive, built-in lighting is an important safety feature by night. The spa acts as a dividing element between raised and lowered portions of this much-used patio environment, complete with an outdoor kitchen. *Courtesy of Aquatic Pools, Inc.*

An artful frame around an inviting blue spa incorporates decorative brick and stone-work. This mini-resort occupies the corner of a small, privately walled backyard. *Courtesy of Aquatic Pools, Inc.*

Brick steps lead up to an artfully raised, half-moon spa at the far side of an expansive swimming pool. *Courtesy of Geremia Pools, Inc.*

A vanishing edge pool allows for an unblemished look at an amazing vista, while a slightly elevated spa trumps the view. *Courtesy of Geremia Pools, Inc.*

Raised above a flagstone patio and tucked neatly into a corner of this stone home, a half-octagon spa is also a scenic pond for those gazing out from within. *Courtesy of Artistic Pools, Inc.*

Stone coping color coordinates with decking, combining for soft effect with a modified rectangular spa. *Courtesy of Hollandia Pools & Spas*

A modified rectangle snuggles into the framework created in meandering stone hardscaping. *Courtesy of Memphis Pool Supply Company*

Rough hewn stone surround creates the illusion of an ancient Roman bath,
but within hydro jets and temperature control are purely 21st century.
Courtesy of Memphis Pool Supply Company

An expansive spa — 5 by 9 feet — is 5 feet deep in the center. It creates a
central gathering spot between upper and lower areas of this small, urban lawn.
Courtesy of Hollandia Pools & Spas

Elevated above a flagstone patio, a 5 x 7 foot spa-was finished with ceramic tile on the interior. *Courtesy of Hollandia Pools & Spas*

A frothy hot spa offers an inviting soak poolside. *Courtesy of Gib-San Pools, Ltd.*

Privacy fence, adorned by trellis-work, surrounds a bubbling hydro-therapy spa.
Courtesy of Gib-San Pools, Ltd.

Stone surrounds a blue wishing well, where muscle aches magically disappear. *Courtesy of Gib-San Pools, Ltd.*

A covered courtyard area shelters a square spa. All of the square architectural details combine in a carefully thought-out plan, resulting in elegant effect. *Courtesy of Alka Pool Construction, Ltd.*

A remote control unit in the home can be used to activate the heating elements and pumps. Another, mounted on the surround, offers on-site temperature control. *Courtesy of Olympic Pools & Spas*

A hot tub sits flush in an expansive, aggregate concrete patio.
Courtesy of Gym & Swim

A spa nests amidst an elaborate framework of stone wall and steps. *Courtesy of Gib-San Pools, Ltd.*

A seaside spa offers hydro-therapy seating for up to eight occupants. *Courtesy of Gib-San Pools, Ltd.*

Tucked into a corner, a bubbling spa is integrated with the pool waters beyond. *Courtesy of Rizzo Pool Construction Co.*

Viewpoints

Left & above:
A tile-lined spa provides submerged seating overlooking an inlet.
Courtesy of Alka Pool Construction, Ltd.

A gulf-front spa is set off by stunning red brick surround. *Courtesy of Rainey Pool Company*

Geometrical shapes merge in an altar to relaxation. *Courtesy of Vaughan Pools & Spas*

Stone steps summon the weary to a circular spa. *Courtesy of Shasta Pools & Spas*

A vanishing edge creates a conversation piece for this little blue desert gem. *Courtesy of Mission Pools*

A squarely centered spa overlooks a pool, an enlarged reflection of itself. *Courtesy of Geremia Pools, Inc.*

A circular spa cuts a neat form within the natural edges of pool and flagstones.
Courtesy of Shasta Pools & Spas

A free-form shape mimics nature's waterway beyond.
Courtesy of Shasta Pools & Spas

A raised hot-tub platform also provides ringside seating, so those staying dry on the barstools can communicate with those soaking. *Courtesy of Gym & Swim*

A hot tub commands the view in a multi-tiered deck setting.
Courtesy of Gym & Swim

Like offerings, planter bowls mark the four corners of a simple, square spa. *Courtesy of Shasta Pools & Spas*

A custom spa takes the high ground in a luxurious backyard landscape.
Courtesy of Shasta Pools & Spas

Indoor Spas

A hospital spa incorporates size and safety features to offer hydro-therapy for multiple patients. *Courtesy of JABCO, Inc.*

A tile deck surrounds this attractive square spa in an attractive sunroom addition. *Courtesy of Hollandia Pools & Spas*

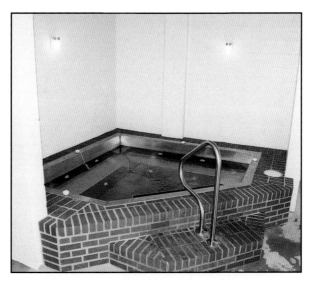

A custom spa was neatly tucked into a corner, with safety railing for access. Seating is possible on all sides, with the wall for leaning against, in addition to the submerged bench. *Courtesy of Memphis Pool Supply Company*

A teardrop shape characterizes an indoor spa. Gilded faucets were installed for easy refills, and cascading waterfall effect. *Courtesy of JABCO, Inc.*

Outdoors is imitated inside, where a spa overlooks water features on both sides. Overflow from the spa, when not in use, creates a waterfall special effect. *Courtesy of Hollandia Pools & Spas*

Stone mosaic work makes for a beautiful spa surround in this compact spa room. *Courtesy of JABCO, Inc.*

A spa broaches indoor and out, with a spillover chute that connects with the pool beyond. *Courtesy of JABCO, Inc.*

A sunroom is dedicated to its central spa. *Courtesy of Rizzo Pool Construction Co.*

A massive spa seats a dozen comfortably, offering all a magnificent view. *Courtesy of Rizzo Pool Construction Co.*

Rock walls offer a man-made cave wherein warm waters and electric-powered jets beckon. *Courtesy of Gib-San Pools, Ltd.*

A keyhole-shaped spa graces an inviting sunroom. *Courtesy of Gib-San Pools, Ltd.*

A commercial hot tub provides warm, soft seating in a shiny setting of polished marble. *Courtesy of Gym & Swim*

Blue hues are a classic choice to line a spa. *Courtesy of Gib-San Pools, Ltd.*

Rock, wood, and foliage bring nature indoors, where a spa steams up this tropical retreat. *Courtesy of Gib-San Pools, Ltd.*

An indoor spa becomes one of the art forms in a tub room dedicated to good taste. *Courtesy of Gib-San Pools, Ltd.*

Ready to be filled, a sunken spa sits flush with floor level windows, which reflect the owner's penchant for candlelight by night. *Courtesy of Gib-San Pools, Ltd.*

A floral shape establishes seating areas around a bean-shaped, sunken center – an artful water attraction within a cozy sunroom. *Courtesy of Gib-San Pools, Ltd.*

Tiled waves spaced along stairs characterize the classical shape of pool and spa within an amazing indoor swim room. A mosaic on the floor isn't lost on the observer, who can mount a balcony for an overview of the scene. *Courtesy of Gib-San Pools, Ltd.*

Natural rocks divide spa from pool, and create an aura of natural formation within this indoor Eden. *Courtesy of Gib-San Pools, Ltd.*

Flagstone and foliage create an outdoor paradise inside. *Courtesy of High-Tech Pools, Inc.*

Water Scapes

A raised square of spa adds punctuation to a pool that vanishes into a natural stone and foliage border. *Courtesy of Mission Pools*

Spa waters spill through a rock border and cascade into the pool beyond in this luxurious backyard landscape. *Courtesy of Riverbend Pools*

An octagonal spa nips into the corner of a long stretch of cool blue pool.
Courtesy of Mission Pools

Natural rock imitates natural formations in a man-made oasis of swimming/soaking pleasure.
Courtesy of Memphis Pool Supply Company

A commercial hot-tub is integrated into a brick and concrete environment designed for outdoor living. *Courtesy of Memphis Pool Supply Company*

A carefully thought out and planned environment leads off with a bubbling spa, and tapers out via a waterfall into a naturally wooded hillside. *Courtesy of Mission Pools*

A cedar trellis shelters a 6 1/2-foot spa. *Courtesy of Hollandia Pools & Spas*

A spa was centered pool-side to add visual variety to a pool-scape. *Courtesy of Memphis Pool Supply Company*

A circular spa is nestled in the curve of a free-form pool. *Courtesy of Hollandia Pools & Spas*

Tile defines the outer limits of a spa, half-in, half-out of the pool. *Courtesy of Memphis Pool Supply Company*

A spa is the first stop upon entering this expansive outdoor environment. *Courtesy of Memphis Pool Supply Company*

Bench seating around a pool edge also serves as step into or from a spa.
Courtesy of Vaughan Pools & Spas

Set just beyond sliding glass doors, location makes this spa an easy dip into the outdoors.
Courtesy of Gib-San Pools, Ltd.

A horseshoe-shaped spa shares billing with a vanishing-edge pool and an outdoor firepit in this patio. *Courtesy of Shasta Pools & Spas*

A circular spa spills over for effect and practical filtration. *Courtesy of Shasta Pools & Spas*

Sky blue within terra cotta tones is magical when lit by twilight. *Courtesy of Shasta Pools & Spas*

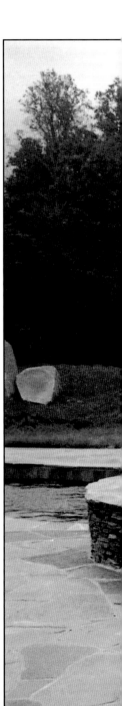

A spa is cunningly integrated into a rock and water landscape.
Courtesy of Master Pools by Paul Haney

A circular spa fits naturally into hardscaping that defies straight lines. *Courtesy of Madison Swimming Pool Company, Inc.*

Rock rings a raised spa overlooking a free-form pool and an amazing wall of falling water. *Courtesy of Meredith Swimming Pool Company*

An amazing feat technically, this spa spills over on all sides when not in use. When hydro-therapy is in order, it quickly heats up and warm jets are activated. *Courtesy of Mission Pools*

A series of interconnected decks includes several wonderful water features, including a water fountain, a waterfall, and a bubbling hot tub. *Courtesy of Gym & Swim*

A spa culminates two dramatic vanishing edges in a water-scape perfectly suited to its home.
Courtesy of Gym & Swim

Here's a little secret the property owners can keep to themselves – a hydrotherapy spa is disguised amidst a running stream, waterfall, and rock pool. *Courtesy of Geremia Pools, Inc.*

Sandstone-colored concrete surround creates a pastel frame for light blue waters. A bubbling hydrotherapy spa offers many levels of comfort within its spacious 47-square-foot area. Beyond, a two-tiered waterfall cascades into the pool. *Courtesy of Geremia Pools, Inc.*

Below:
A circular spa creates an area of interest, balancing an eye-catching arbor of arches. *Courtesy of Geremia Pools, Inc.*

Set amidst a series of water-features – a running stream and a natural, rock-edged swimming pool, this kidney shaped spa seems part of a natural landscape. However, the alluring features – jet massage, warm waters, and automatic control system — are all products of the latest technology. *Courtesy of Creative Master Pools*

Shapes are orchestrated for classic effect in these two examples of overall water- and hard-scape, the centerpieces being the circular spas. *Courtesy of The Clearwater Company, Inc.*

Contemporary flair characterizes a pool, ending in an exclamation point at a square spa.
Courtesy of The Clearwater Company, Inc.

Water Features

A waterfall cascades from a semi-circular wall, adding to the effect of swirling hot waters in this soothing spa. *Courtesy of Custom Pools & Patios, Inc.*

Water gushes forth from an arched wall of harlequin-pattern stone, spilling from catch basin to spa beyond. *Courtesy of Sun & Swim Pools, Inc.*

A spa is cleverly disguised as a waterfall; a mesmerizing magnet that is the focal point of a small, enclosed garden. *Courtesy of Keith Zars Pools*

A water fountain provides visual and aural backdrop for a spa with one matching jet.
Courtesy of Riverbend Pools

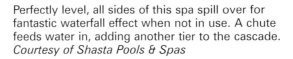

Perfectly level, all sides of this spa spill over for fantastic waterfall effect when not in use. A chute feeds water in, adding another tier to the cascade.
Courtesy of Shasta Pools & Spas

Outdoor space was minimal, but comfort wasn't spared — a corner was dedicated to a custom spa, complete with fountain for added eye appeal.
Courtesy of Memphis Pool Supply Company

Blue waters and orange stucco act as stage settings for a dramatic waterfall effect. This hydro-therapy spa is the patio's main feature presentation, even when no one is soaking in it.
Courtesy of Alka Pool Construction, Ltd.

Spa and waterfall light up by night, both forming lovers' retreats at any time.
Courtesy of Aqua Blue Pools

Twilight smiles on an appealing garden, where a lit fountain marks the spot for soothing spa waters.
Courtesy of Pool Tech Midwest, Inc.

A circular spa is integrated with the pool waters when not in use.
Courtesy of Shasta Pools & Spas

A cascade of water falls into, another from, a spa when not in use. *Courtesy of Mission Pools*

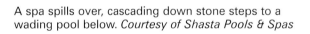

A spa spills over, cascading down stone steps to a wading pool below. *Courtesy of Shasta Pools & Spas*

Zen-like in its appearance within a flat concrete landscape, a rock waterfall overlooks the spare forms of spa and pool. *Courtesy of Shasta Pools & Spas*

Opposing page:
Rocks add points of interest among the meandering lines of spa and pool. *Courtesy of Shasta Pools & Spas*

Black adds allure to a spa, where a symphony of falling water plays against a mountain backdrop. *Courtesy of Shasta Pools & Spas*

Part of a waterfall attraction, an elevated spa is the jewel in a waterscape crown. *Courtesy of Riverbend Pools*

River stones adorn a spa, part of a
series of waterfalls beside a pool.
Courtesy of Riverbend Pools

A raised spa adds a splash of water, and a splash of color, poolside. *Courtesy of New Bern Pool*

A half-moon spa spills into inviting blue pool waters. *Courtesy of New Bern Pool*

A fountain adds a focal point of interest to a spa while providing the relaxing sound of falling water. The raised spa extends patio seating without creating the clutter of chairs or lounges in the spa area. *Courtesy of Aquatic Pools, Inc.*

The raised spa with glass block and fountain create a visual centerpiece from the front door, with lighting effects added for nighttime viewing.

A spray of fountain casts classical elegance to a spa, perfect for this carefully tended garden setting. *Courtesy of Sandler Pools*

A clover is an attractive spa built for four, with a central fountain and therapeutic jets. *Courtesy of New Bern Pool*

Water falls from rocks, concealing the presence of a hot spa above. *Courtesy of Prestige Pools & Spas, Inc.*

Fountain and waterfall disguise the modern conveniences of a soothing spa. On the far side of the fountain, you can make out the automated vacuum at work on the bottom. *Courtesy of Gib-San Pools, Ltd.*

A fountain bubbles out of the center of a spa, creating a circle of falling water within the confines of the raised body. A cutout allows one side of the spa to spillover into the surrounding pool. *Courtesy of Artistic Pools, Inc.*

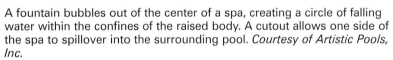

A jetted swim spa was designed to run hot or cold, as a pool or spa, measuring 9 feet wide by 12 feet long.
Courtesy of Aquatic Pools, Inc.

A spa appears to drain into the creek, which appears to flow into the pool. In fact, multiple water systems are at work, each acting separately. *Courtesy of Vaughan Pools & Spas*

Stonework gives tropical feel to an environment dedicated to water recreation. *Courtesy of Rainey Pool Company*

Below:
A spa in the foreground is sheltered, though not cut off from the pool beyond. *Courtesy of Shasta Pools & Spas*

Brick, patio pavers, and a new circular spa leant new life to an existing pool in this beautiful renovation project. *Courtesy of Rainey Pool Company*

A patio and spa command a broad vista. *Courtesy of Shasta Pools & Spas*

A series of straight walls demarcate gathering areas within one sprawling patio. *Courtesy of Shasta Pools & Spas*

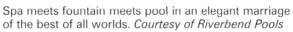

Spa meets fountain meets pool in an elegant marriage of the best of all worlds. *Courtesy of Riverbend Pools*

A spa stands top and center in a multi-level, multi-function water environment. *Courtesy of Riverbend Pools*

A spa is cleverly disguised as a water fountain when not in use.
Courtesy of Geremia Pools, Inc.

Garden Ornaments

A spacious spa sits gemlike amidst a flagstone courtyard patio. *Courtesy of Gib-San Pools, Ltd.*

Steam rises from a custom spa. *Courtesy of Shasta Pools & Spas*

Artful fencing restricts access to a spacious swim spa tucked neatly into a side yard.
Courtesy of Gib-San Pools, Ltd.

Sheltered under a towering stone wall and nestled between planters, a watery blue nest awaits. *Courtesy of Gib-San Pools, Ltd.*

Below:
Set at the end of inviting, oversized flagstone steps, a wishing-well blue spa invites. *Courtesy of Gib-San Pools, Ltd.I*

A raised spa and planters form the focal point at the pinnacle of a long pool.
Courtesy of High-Tech Pools, Inc.

A tile slope separates raised spa and the cooler pool waters beyond.
Courtesy of Gib-San Pools, Ltd.

An outdoor fireplace and lamppost illumine a cobalt blue spa by night.
Courtesy of Gib-San Pools, Ltd.

A spa is sheltered by trellis and massive boulders, resulting in a private, cave-like environment.
Courtesy of Shasta Pools & Spas

An arbor caps a raised patio with a sunken spa at its center. Stamped and colored concrete imitates natural flagstone. *Courtesy of Terry Pool Company, Inc.*

An attractive pavilion shelters a custom spa/fountain. *Courtesy of Shasta Pools & Spas*

A spa is tucked into a garden nook. *Courtesy of Sun & Swim Pools, Inc.*

A rounded curb between spa and pool offers a comfortable place to lounge and sun, half-in, half-out of cool or hot waters. *Courtesy of Shasta Pools & Spas*

Lighting varies the landscape by day and night. Here it ushers out twilight while the spa heats up for a late-night soak. *Courtesy of Patio Pools of Tucson, Inc.*

Concrete artfully imitates stone, in an artfully enclosed area hewn out specifically for a sunken hot tub. The intimate spa is part of a larger water-scape created for a rural backyard. Behind wrought-iron furniture, a speaker sits cleverly disguised as a rock, part of an overall outdoor sound system. *Courtesy of Gym & Swim*

A rock waterfall spills into a spa, reached in this walled-in oasis of green by a series of enormous stepping stones. *Courtesy of Aquatic Pools, Inc.*

Enormous in size, this spa doubles as lap pool. An exerciser might swim into a jet for a muscle-toning workout, then crank up the heat and return an hour later for a muscle relaxing soak. *Courtesy of Gib-San Pools, Ltd.*

Spa, pool, and hammock add up to an idyll almost anyone could afford. The waterfront property, however, might elude the masses. *Courtesy of Gib-San Pools, Ltd.*

By lining this square spa with black finish, a reflecting pool is created. In addition to a melodious waterfall, and a surround of attractive statuary, this dip offers occupants soothing hydro-therapy. *Courtesy of Gib-San Pools, Ltd.*

A waterfall cascades into a circular spa. Besides circulating the water, the pump also keeps the spa sparkling clean. *Courtesy of Gib-San Pools, Ltd.*

Tucked close to home, amidst a natural rock garden, this enchanting spa is a stone's step away for those in need of a candle-lit soak. *Courtesy of Geremia Pools, Inc.*

An expansive, kidney shaped spa beckons, complete with a stair-stepped rock waterfall at the furthermost reaches of a thoughtfully hard-scaped backyard. *Courtesy of Creative Master Pools*

A corner of a man-made pond/pool is temperature-controlled on demand, for those who want to warm their bones while enjoying an incredible view, seemingly created by Mother Nature herself. *Courtesy of Artistic Pools, Inc.*

Below:
A bubbling spa is set neatly into terraced, flower-strewn corner carefully hewed into a steep hillside. An automatic cover keeps the waters clean when not in use. *Courtesy of Custom Pools & Patios, Inc.*

A columned, neo-classical crown caps a round spa, complete with spillover
for waterfall effect when not in use. *Courtesy of Barrington Pools, Inc.*

A lagoon-style beachfront hydro-therapy spa is 8 by 14 feet. The natural rock waterfall
operates on a separate pump so the jets and fall can operate separately or at the same time.

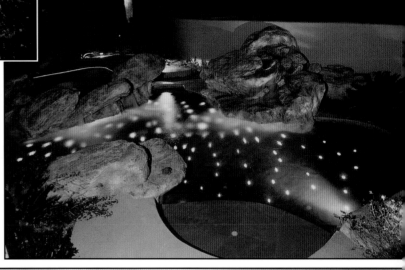

By night, light effects add excitement to pool and spa.
Courtesy of Patio Pools of Tucson, Inc.

Like the contemporary home beyond, the square sides of this spa are softened by natural forms in the landscaping. *Courtesy of Patio Pools of Tucson, Inc.*

A bridge connects home and remote, private patio, where a bubbling hot spa furnishes the ultimate getaway.
Courtesy of New Bern Pool

Resource Guide

Alka Pool Construction, Ltd.
4013 Graveley Street
Burnaby, BC Canada V5C 3T5
604-320-2552
www.alkapools.com

Aqua Blue Pools
7332 Peppermill Parkway
N. Charleston, SC 29418
843-767-7665
6 Nichols Court
Hilton Head Island, SC 29926
843-689-6056
www.aquabluepools.net

Aquatic Pools, Inc.
106 Industrial Park Loop NE
Rio Rancho, NM 87124
505-991-3681

Artistic Pools, Inc.
3884 N. Peachtree Road
Atlanta, GA 30341
770-458-9177
www.artisticpools.com

Barrington Pools, Inc.
PO Box 3906
Barrington, IL 60011
847-381-1245
www.barrington-pools.com

The Clearwater Company, Inc.
1682 Lake Murray Blvd.
Columbia, S.C. 29212
803-781-8364
www.clearwaterco.com

Creative Master Pools
537 Commerce Street
Franklin Lakes, NJ 07417
201-337-7600
www.creativemasterpools.com

Custom Pools & Patios, Inc.
4048 Chinden Blvd.
Boise, ID 83714
208-345-2792
www.custompoolsandpatio.com

Geremia Pools, Inc.
1327 65th St.
Sacramento, CA 95819
916-914-7800
www.geremiapools.com
sales@geremiapools.com

Gib-San Pools, Ltd.
59 Milvan
Toronto, Ontario Canada M9L 1Y8
416-749-4361
www.GibSanPools.com

Gym & Swim, "A Master Pool Builder"
8130 New LaGrange Rd.
Louisville, KY 40222
502-426-1326
www.gymandswim.com

High-Tech Pools, Inc.
31333 Industrial Parkway
Cleveland, OH 44070
440-979-5070
www.hightechpools.com

Hollandia Pools & Spas
1891 Wharncliffe Road S.
London, Ontario, Canada N6L 1K2
519-652-3257
www.hollandiagardens.com

JABCO, Inc. Master Pools
807 Missouri Street
Tuscumbia, AL 35674
256-381-2861
www.jabcopools.com

Keith Zars Pools
17427 San Pedro
San Antonio, TX 78232
210-494-0800

Madison Swimming Pool Company, Inc.
1416 Dickerson Road
Goodlettsville, TN 37072
615-865-2964
www.madisonpools.com

Maryland Pools, Inc.
9515 Gerwig Lane, Suite 119
Columbia, MD 21046
410-995-6600
301-621-3319
11166 Main Street, Suite 402
Fairfax, VA 22030
703-359-7192
www.mdpools.com

Master Pools® Guild, Inc.
9607 Gayton Road, Suite 200
Richmond, VA 23233
800-392-3044
www.masterpoolsguild.com

Master Pools by New Bern Pool
5205 Capital Blvd.
Raleigh, NC 276164
919-873-1777
www.newbernpool.com

Master Pools by Paul Haney, Inc.
1240 North Kelsey Street
Visalia, CA 93291
559-651-1177
www.masterpoolsvisalia.com

Memphis Pool Supply Company
2762 Getwell Road
Memphis, TN 38118
901-365-2480
www.memphispool.com

Meredith Swimming Pool Company
116 Stagecoach Trail
Greensboro, NC 27409
336-299-7044
www.meredithpools.com

Mission Pools
755 W. Grand Avenue
Escondido, CA 92025
760-743-2605
www.missionpools.com

Olympic Pools & Spas
801 Coliseum Blvd. West
Fort Wayne, IN 46808
260-482-7665
www.poolnspa.com

Panama Pools of N.W. Florida
291 Powell Adams Road
Panama City, FL 32413
850-233-0950
www.panamapoolsandspas.com

Paradise Pools & Spas
4221 Division Street
Metairie, LA 70002
504-888-0505
www.paradisepools.com

Patio Pools of Tucson, Inc.
7960 E. 22nd St.
Tucson, AZ 85710
520-886-1211
www.patiopoolsaz.com

Pool Tech Midwest, Inc.
3233 First Avenue S.E.
Cedar Rapids, IO 52402
319-365-8609
www.pooltech.com

Prestige Pools & Spas, Inc.
P.O. Box 2224
Edmond, OK 73083
405-340-7665
wedigpools@msn.com

Rainey Pool Company
1101 Gulf Freeway
League City, TX 77573
281-338-1555
www.raineypools.com

Riverbend Pools
4016 West Plano Pkwy., Suite 100
Plano, TX 75093
972-596-7393
www.riverbendpools.com

Rizzo Pool Construction Co.
388 Stamm Road
Newington, CT 06111
860-667-2214
www.rizzopools.com

Sandler Pools
4016 W. Plano Pkwy., Suite 100
Plano, TX 75093
972-596-7393
www.sandlerpools.com

Shasta Pools & Spas
6031 North 16th Street
Phoenix, AZ 85016
602-532-3750
www.shastapools.com

Sun & Swim Pools, Inc.
3910 West Main Street
Grandview, MO 64030
816-761-7665
www.sunandswimpools.com

Terry Pool Company, Inc.
10350 North Michigan Road
Carmel, IN 46032
317-872-2502
317-879-1034 Fax
terrypools@aol.com
www.terrypools.com

Vaughan Pools & Spas
1909 South Country Club Drive
Jefferson City, MO 65109
573-893-3650
www.vaughanpools.com